BARNET
THEN & NOW

IN COLOUR

Yasmine Webb

The
History
Press

First published in 2013

The History Press
The Mill, Brimscombe Port
Stroud, Gloucestershire, GL5 2QG
www.thehistorypress.co.uk

British Library Cataloguing in Publication Data.
A catalogue record for this book is available from the British Library.

ISBN 978 0 7524 8832 5

Typesetting and origination by The History Press
Printed in India.

CONTENTS

ACKNOWLEDGEMENTS

Barnet Museum, p.22 Highland House and p.25 The Potteries; Frederick Ian Crook, p.68 People's Dispensary for Sick Animals (PDSA); John Heathfield, p.65 The Chapel; Friern Barnet & District Local History Society, p.38 Rising Sun; L.B. of Enfield, Local Studies Library & Archives, p.34 Osidge; and Benjamin Perl for permission to photograph The Pillar Hotel, p.71 St Saviour's Home. These contributors have kindly given permission for the use of their photographs.

To the many people interested in portraying the best of what the borough represents, whose knowledge of the area contributes to this publication.

The older photos are from the Borough of Barnet Local Studies Collection; the recent photographs are by the author.

INTRODUCTION

Barnet is an area of considerable topographical contrast, from the highest points of Barnet Town and Mill Hill in the north to a gradual descent east and west forming spectacular landscapes and valleys. It has captured artists' imagination well into the twentieth century, when, like many parts of London, it began to accelerate its physical development. It is difficult to condense the residential attractions that drew so many to it into this selection. However, I hope these pictures will give a flavour of what the borough is truly like.

Economically it was an agricultural area that by the early nineteenth century, was providing hay for the horse-drawn transport services that prevailed at the time. It was also a most attractive place for retiring gentleman, those of considerable wealth and the industrious new elite. Places such as Hadley and Hendon took their place in this arrangement and many houses were built reflecting this background. With time, certain areas strengthened in particular services, Hendon, geographically the largest by 1910, was an aeronautical centre which was culturally engaging the young and influential. Flight, at the time, was an attraction which engaged the curiosity also of non-technicians, and was then a rare experience. The manufacturing developments mainly hugged the Edgware Road from Cricklewood to Edgware town where companies such as Grahame White Ltd, Airco (Aeronautical Manufacturing Company Ltd), Handley Page, de Havilland Aircraft Company and many more joined the providers associated with flying.

One important attraction was the direct communication with central London, the other was the fact that London was growing, and more space was needed for building and testing large technological products. The growth in housing pushed out this industry, which was now considered too near to residential habitation. Today the only evidence of a once-mighty employer is the Royal Air Force on the former Grahame White's space.

The authorities that collectively formed the new London Borough of Barnet brought topographic, economic and cultural contributions that strengthened what each area had to offer in terms of house and home. Barnet was carved from the former counties of Middlesex and Hertfordshire as part of an enlarged London. This placed additional administrative complexities particularly relating to identifying boundaries. Train communication made tremendous inroads and opened up the borough further as an attractive place. The first railway came to New Barnet in 1850 but had minimal impact for a number of years; the tube line made a much greater impression.

The former authorities of Barnet, East Barnet, Finchley, Friern Barnet and Hendon bring ancient histories to the story of the borough, but by focusing on the visible changes that many people can recognise today I have referred mainly to the last few centuries. Barnet remains a highly desirable residential area that has retained much of its architectural charm, tinctured with large green spaces and a cultural mix that brings new ideas to its community.

BARNET COLLEGE, WOOD STREET

THIS SITE OPENED as the Queen Elizabeth's Boys School. It was founded by Royal Charter in 1573, and housed in the old Tudor Hall (which still stands beside today's rebuilt Barnet College, opened in late 2010). It was one of the earliest schools established in England, commanding an excellent position opposite the parish church

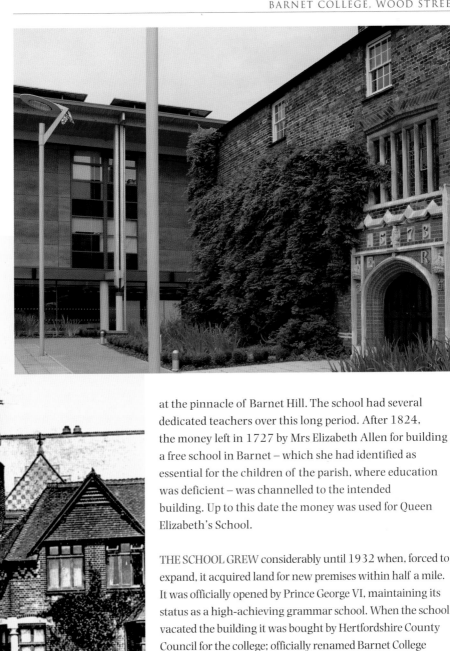

at the pinnacle of Barnet Hill. The school had several dedicated teachers over this long period. After 1824, the money left in 1727 by Mrs Elizabeth Allen for building a free school in Barnet – which she had identified as essential for the children of the parish, where education was deficient – was channelled to the intended building. Up to this date the money was used for Queen Elizabeth's School.

THE SCHOOL GREW considerably until 1932 when, forced to expand, it acquired land for new premises within half a mile. It was officially opened by Prince George VI, maintaining its status as a high-achieving grammar school. When the school vacated the building it was bought by Hertfordshire County Council for the college; officially renamed Barnet College in 1963, and rebuilt twice on this site, it still does credit to its illustrious history. In 1876 the London Society for the Extension of University Teaching began to utilise the Barnet Centre, and lectures were held at various places. The education at this site continues to be challenging today, as in the past. The site is still growing, and the college is still providing popular courses today.

METHODIST CHURCH, HIGH STREET

THE CHAPEL WAS built in 1892 as a new site for the Methodists, who moved from a chapel a little north from this site at Hadley. It took a prominent place in Barnet High Street. The generosity of Miss Wyburn of Hadley Manor enabled its building and she appears on the foundation stone, laid on 21 May 1891. Just a few years after this photograph was taken in 1989, the church was assigned for demolition.

THE NEW DESIGN, a pedestrian walkway with mostly small shop units, was constructed by Essex, Goodman & Suggitt. The attractive twin towers were to have a significant impact on the design of The Spires, as the shopping precinct was to be called. The precinct contains a number of small businesses stretching from the High Street to the back (fronting Stapylton Road, where a large Waitrose supermarket stands). The whole complex is nicely designed, with café seating and an opening along the centre giving it a spacious feel. Today, The Spires is still the main shopping centre for the area, and houses considerable choice concentrated within a limited space.

THE GATE, ARKLEY

PREVIOUSLY KNOWN AS the Old Bell, The Gate was rebuilt to serve customers working for the brick trade in the surrounding Barnet Common. Both the Arkley Windmill, opposite, and Brickfield Lane are a residue of development around this trade. In the early 1841 census, terraces within yards of the pub and cottages on the Glebeland nearby were occupied by brick-makers who had migrated to Barnet after 1830. A fascinating enclosure map of 1817 shows the Old Bell in the occupation of Peter Clutterbuck, who held numerous public houses in Barnet. Even the public house was run by members of the extended brick-making families. A sign in the shape of a gate stands above the Old Bell, just as it does today, the signpost a reminder of the gated area that was once the entrance to the common, the limit for containing cattle (according to the common's custom).

THE AREA HAD several ponds, caused by surface clay digging rather than a watery landscape. This whole area was associated with brick-making in the nineteenth century. The Brick Layers' Arms, Arkley, was a beerhouse from the 1850s. By the 1930s it was an off-licence near the Three Elms's intersection at the far end of this same road. John Williams is listed in the 1756 War Office survey as a provider of lodging and provisions for billeted soldiers. It was an important stop for travellers on the very edge of Barnet's parish boundary, and looks back to an even earlier date than the eighteenth century.

THE PHYSIC WELL, WELL ROAD

A NEW SPA town was anticipated when a spring in the grounds of a farm on Barnet Common was first mentioned in print in 1650. The diarist Samuel Pepys, Celia Fiennes and Daniel Defoe all wrote of taking the waters – with mixed experiences. One problem was the spring's isolated position: being 1 mile away from the town centre, carriage provision was necessary; a carriage keeper was therefore engaged. Developing the waters

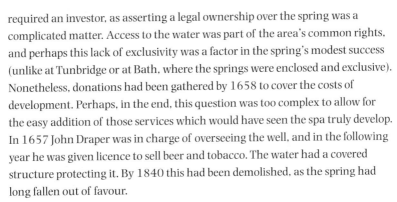

required an investor, as asserting a legal ownership over the spring was a complicated matter. Access to the water was part of the area's common rights, and perhaps this lack of exclusivity was a factor in the spring's modest success (unlike at Tunbridge or at Bath, where the springs were enclosed and exclusive). Nonetheless, donations had been gathered by 1658 to cover the costs of development. Perhaps, in the end, this question was too complex to allow for the easy addition of those services which would have seen the spa truly develop. In 1657 John Draper was in charge of overseeing the well, and in the following year he was given licence to sell beer and tobacco. The water had a covered structure protecting it. By 1840 this had been demolished, as the spring had long fallen out of favour.

WHEN THE LAND was being developed by Barnet Council in the 1920s into Wellhouse estate, the well was re-discovered and developed as a feature of the new estate. They excavated the older well chamber, which was found to be in perfect condition. A mock-Tudor cover was built in 1937, conserving one of the few original chambers to have survived. A major hospital, formerly the local workhouse, stood nearby, and was redeveloped in 2003. It was said to have been the inspiration for the workhouse in Dicken's *Oliver Twist*, and his setting of the meeting with the Artful Dodger in Barnet. Preserved with its cover, and surrounded by a green space, the spring is still on a road to nowhere. These residential premises are to its advantage, however, its historical importance is still little recognised by the wider world.

SALISBURY ARMS, HIGH STREET

THIS LARGE AND modern 1928 mock-Tudor house was quite a feature in the High Street when it was built, replacing a Georgian inn on the same site. It blended in well, and was certainly ornate: it was set back from the road, giving it a certain grace, and was very actively used for community events. The previous inns on this site went by an assortment of names: The Tabar, in 1557, had become the Tabar and Pipe by 1753; the building was thereafter known as the Royal Waggon until 1828. A new name was then decided upon after Lord Salisbury stayed at the inn in around 1821 – no doubt tempted by the establishment's preferential rates, which offered him post horses at three pence a mile cheaper than the Red Lion or Green Man. It became the Salisbury Arms in his honour.

IN 1901 THE Barnet Amicables – who had held their social meetings, since 1780, at the Red Lion inn – changed their patronage to the Salisbury Arms. The new building was called the Salisbury Hotel. Arthur Fisher was the landlord from the 1930s to 1968, a notably long occupancy. The inn was demolished in 1988, to make way for the modern shops of the era. The building is today occupied by Iceland.

THE THREE ELMS, ARKLEY

A STRATEGIC SITE at the centre of the thoroughfare, where two roads divide on an open plain, will always attract travellers; the Three Elms was an isolated, robust and functional building in the nineteenth century. It was rebuilt, in the 1890s, on the site of a small public house named after the Three Elms Farm (whose windows once overlooked a gibbet for highwaymen caught on Barnet Common). Highwayman were hung and their bodies left on view as a warning to transgressors of their impending fate should they be caught. Political and economic instability provided many opportunities for highway robbery in the eighteenth century, when incidents were rife. There was no effective county police force, save one to two local constables, until

the extension of the Metropolitan Police force in 1829 by Sir Robert Peel. The area covered by this force then grew to cover the area beyond Greater London (and similarly the Hertfordshire Constabulary in 1841).

THE ADJACENT ROAD was called Gallows Lane until local residents objected; the site was then renamed 'Galley Lane'. By 1879 it was owned by Mrs Sedgwick, from the brewery family of the same name, but the licensee was John Toone, who changed the pub's name in 1896 and whose name sits above the entrance door. It remains today as The Arkley, a flourishing popular public house with outside seating, albeit with a considerable extension to the premises.

ELIZABETH ALLEN'S SCHOOL, WOOD STREET

IN 1727 MRS Elizabeth Allen had left money for building
a free school in Barnet for boys and girls, but it was not
built till 1824 as the money was diverted to the Queen
Elizabeth's Boys' Grammar School. In 1823 the rector of
East and Chipping Barnet, Dr David Garrow, who was also
the governor of Queen Elizabeth's Grammar School and
who lived at Hadley at the end of Barnet town, insisted the
money be used for the original purpose. The awareness of
the importance of education in improving opportunities
for parishioners was growing, but it was admirable that
Dr Garrow recognised this need. Some finance from the
National Society and subscriptions from residents enabled
its opening.

IN 1945 IT became a secondary school. The school closed in 1973. Today the building is a retirement home, having retained the original edifice fronting Wood Street but expanding considerably on that, with modern flats and car park behind.

THE RECTORY, No. 61 WOOD STREET

IN 1890, THE Rectory was built by the Ecclesiastical Commissioners for England on land donated by the Byng family. Its position on a corner site facing Ravenscroft Park was an added attraction, with Elizabeth Allen's School as its neighbour. The first occupant was

D.W. Barrett, rector of Chipping Barnet until 1910. The property was sold by Reverend Dean, rector of Chipping Barnet, in 1936, to Barnet Urban District Council (for use as council offices). It was used as a Social Services' area office in the 1970s, and subsequently became redundant. It was rebuilt and enlarged in around the year 2000, retaining part of the frontage, and developed into flats. In 1817 the field was owned by Robert Tapster, church warden; it then contained over 3 acres, to which he added the frontage of Wood Street when he purchased that too, along with the twenty-two perches (a now obsolete measurement of land) which appear on the 1817 Inclosure Map.

TODAY A ROAD is named after Tapster in the High Street, Barnet. It was there by around 1830, and is shown in the 1841 Tithes Redemption map. The house was called 'Ravenscroft', after the park opposite, by 1951.

HIGHLAND HOUSE, ABBOTTS ROAD

A LARGE VICTORIAN house, with gardens of a considerable size, was built for Joseph Bevan Braithwaite by architects Messers Clark and Moscrop of Darlington. Bevan Braithwaite lived here with his wife Martha Gillett and his nine children. He trained as a barrister but, due to a distinct stammer, he did not practice in court. Instead, Braithwaite, born into a Quaker family, became a Quaker minister; his wife was also a Quaker minister. Braithwaite was a keen astronomer and set up an observatory, building a copper dome in his house (visible in the photograph). This was a rare occurrence as very few observatories

were built – despite the topography of the borough, which was conducive to this interest, Barnet being one of two of the highest points of the borough. He invested in designing a garden that adorns Highland's today and is one of the most hidden and charming of public parks designed and built by James Pulham & Son, landscape designers. The park was bought by East Barnet Urban District Council – a magnificent purchase for the borough, with gardens that, although modest, give an impression of considerable size.

THE HOUSE WAS demolished in 1972 and a block of flats that overlooks the enclosed gardens command a lovely view.

THE POTTERIES, MAYS LANE

ON THIS SITE was a common, weather-boarded lodging house called 'the Potteries', seen here in the 1930s. The building was owned by Herbert Verinder. The Verinder family were also associated with pottery in Arkley, north of this site, another area for clay and kilns. By the late nineteenth century mostly brick work was undertaken, as the amount of housing was expanding; however, the company also had a side-line in making ornamental pots for the surrounding enclosed gardens, for which there was a growing demand. At an earlier time, in around 1817, a large building on the site was owned by St Andrew's, Holborn, believed to be a home for children. (It was common for institutions to use outer

London areas to reduce costs, and to provide ample fresh air.) There were several care houses of this type in the eighteenth and nineteenth century, including The Foundling Hospital children's home, opened in 1764 in Hadley Road. The Foundling Hospital's main home was in London, but it branched out to several districts outside the city.

THE SITE HAS a long history of pottery. On the opposite side runs Potters' Lane, with a number of centuries of pottery association – as has the surrounding area, though very little evidence of this may be found in local archival documents. (Hertfordshire local studies may have more information, the area being formerly in the County of Hertfordshire.) This house was eventually demolished in around 1951.

LONDON & SOUTH WESTERN BANK LTD, EAST BARNET

SUCH A SPLENDID architectural line as this row winds around the corner between the Triangle and Station Road. The gradation emphasises the Triangle opposite, on which stands an elegant statue on a white obelisk supporting a bronze statue of

the 'Angel of Victory' as a memorial to the First World War. The names of those who fell in the Second World War were later added. There was also a water trough beside the statue, now gone. The bank, the primary business here at the time the first photograph was taken, shows its face to all three angles of the road. The shops and bank were built in 1890, and were the work of more than one architect. One of the men who designed this building was Edward Banks Julian. He was named after Sir Edward Banks, a builder of bridges, dockyards and prisons who Julian's father, an architect and civil engineer, had worked for and much admired. In 1892 the manager of the bank was Walter Small – banking was certainly not a small concern for him in those days.

THE BANK IS now a commercial concern. The statue was erected opposite the East Barnet Town Hall, which, previous to the formation of the Borough of Barnet in 1965, was its own authority and ran all its services. Five former authorities were at that time merged to form the new borough, as happened in many areas around London, to create an extended metropolis.

27

NEW BARNET STATION, THE TRIANGLE, STATION ROAD

THIS STATION, OPENED on 7 August 1850 by the Great Northern Railway for the carriage of goods to and from the North, later opened for passenger transport. There was some conflict between the local landowner, whose isolated mansion on Lyonsdown Estate stood in the grounds of the intended rail line, and the GNR. The whole estate was sold, with some animosity, when the company decided to go ahead with the build; the excess land was sold for development. There was a distinct division on the new estate between the large detached houses on the Lyonsdown side and the small terraced houses built opposite the rail tracks for the use of railway workers. A very modest design for the station served its purpose as a trade station for delivery and collection,

but was less impressive when the station opened to passengers. One highlight in the history of the station was the capture, on film, of a train emerging from the Hadley tunnel towards New Barnet in the 1890s. This scene was captured by local filmmaker and pioneer Birt Acres, and the film was considered innovative and exciting at the time.

THE STATION WAS the first to open in Barnet, driving rail lines through open fields, and was the instigator of house development in the area – though not dramatically at first. There is no frontage today for customers, but there is a very small ticket sales office adjacent to the foot bridge for commuters. The station has recently been cosmetically improved and is now more user-friendly.

SOUTHAW GIRLS SCHOOL, CORNER OF RUSSELL LANE AND CHURCH HILL ROAD

IN THE 1920S this area was completely undeveloped, with large tracks of fields. Then the Cockfosters tube line, which opened in 1933, instigated change. The school pictured here was founded in 1939 for eleven to fourteen year olds. It is surprising to see that the area looks almost fully developed, just six years later.

THE SCHOOL MERGED with Ashmole Boys School in 1971 as a mixed-sex secondary school. In the interim period it was part of Barnet College Adult Education. A private housing scheme thereafter took up what was then a considerable space – it was once a very large school. The older photograph, taken in 1984, shows the extent of its footprint. Ashmole, in New Southgate, lies on the border of Borough of Enfield, serving an enlarged population there. The building was demolished in around 2008.

31

HALLIWICK HOUSE, COLNEY HATCH LANE, FRIERN BARNET

THIS HOUSE WAS rebuilt in 1601, on the site of an older structure, on the west-side junction of Colney Hatch Lane and Woodhouse Road. The ground was landscaped with a boating lake, orchard, kitchen garden and bowling green, all of which had fallen out of use by 1628. The magnificent tree was propped up by wooden spears and planted at the same time as the seventeenth-century rebuild. John Trott was lord of the manor of Halliwick in 1601, succeeding his father, John Trott, to that position. George Crawshay and family resided here since around 1851, often using it as a country home. George was an iron merchant and grandson of the South Wales 'Iron King' William Crawshay. The family of Crawshay's mother, Josephe Louise Dufaud, owned the largest ironworks in France

at Fourchambault. She is seen here seated in a large cane wheelchair, viewing a lazy afternoon's family game of tennis, in around 1880.

THE HOUSE WAS later a girl's school and was demolished in around 1920. Until this time the area was predominantly rural. After the First World War, new building in the area significantly increased its population – and with this came the development of the site, together with a corner block of shops (named Halliwick Parade). Colney Hatch Dry Cleaners' is one of the oldest companies operating here.

OSIDGE, No. 151 CHASE SIDE, EAST BARNET

IN 1893, THIS building was bought by Sir Thomas Lipton, the tea magnate of Lipton's Tea fame. He imported his teas from Sri Lanka (then known as Ceylon). Sir Thomas had a passion for sailing and raced in numerous yachting events. Lipton built his fortune from humble beginnings and always held an annual spree at his home for his employees. The house was decorated to his taste, and the garden provided a range of exotic fruits for

the table: Sir Thomas engaged an expert gardener for his hothouse, where he also cultured orchids. The grounds also contained an ice house. Lipton's family moved to Hutchesontown in Glasgow from Northern Ireland, where he took up a job as cabin boy on the Burns Line between Glasgow and Belfast. He went on to travel to America, Sri Lanka (Ceylon) and other localities. He very quickly acquired marketing skills and returned to Glasgow to run his parent's shop, opening several more over time. He then branched into tea, which was a huge success: there are exotic photographs of him entertaining in his tree house in the garden in Osidge, with Ceylonese servants attending him. Throughout his life he was generous to many causes and left bequests to Glasgow hospitals, servants and friends. The Lipton brand was ultimately acquired by the Unilever Co. Another former occupant, John Hadley, vice president of the Royal Society, had scientific interests. He improved upon a type of telescope designed by Sir Isaac Newton, solving several problems which affected the mirrors and hence making it possible for telescopes to become much larger. The Hadley family held this estate for several generations, up until 1743, when John Hadley died.

THE HOUSE WAS rebuilt and sold in 1808 by Mr John Kingston of Oakhill and in 1834 bought by Augustus Bosanquet. Today the house is a home for retired nurses and must be such a satisfying place in which to live.

ORANGE TREE,
FRIERN BARNET LANE

AN INN HAS been on this site for at least two centuries. In 1817 it was recommended to sportsmen in pursuit of the plentiful wildfowl at Colney Hatch. The inn, standing opposite Halliwick Manor House and situated at the centre of a major crossroad, played a prominent part in the life of the community. For here parish meetings, election of parish officers, auctions, disputes and other necessities were discussed, and the building acted as a centre for the consideration of many issues, as did many inns before the nineteenth century. The building therefore played a prominent part in the life of the community. Before the Reformation this crossroads was the route to Whetstone from Highgate, a circuitous route around Finchley Common (which was not open as a thoroughfare until the fourteenth century). The building was a homely affair and even offered rooms for the traveller in the nineteenth century. In 1850 the second largest mental asylum in the County of Middlesex, Colney Hatch Asylum, had opened. Albert,

the prince consort, laid down the foundation stone. It housed 1,000 inmates and created many jobs in its maintenance which instigated the movement of people into this very rural area. A new railway station, later known as New Southgate, was designed to stop alongside the asylum: they both opened in the same year, and the station was extremely useful to the working of the asylum.

THE ORANGE TREE was rebuilt in 1909 to the design seen today. It proudly proclaims the dates '1595-1909' on the façade, in remembrance of its glory days. It was quite recently converted to a Tesco minimarket, providing added choice for shoppers.

RISING SUN, No. 248
OAKLEIGH ROAD NORTH

A BEERHOUSE HAS been on this site since 1892, when Joseph Bass, beer retailer, held a building on a third of the plot's site. He also held Bass cottages adjacent to it. Building and letting premises for residential occupation was an increasing opportunity

for landlords, catering for tenants moving here for employment. This photograph, from 1950, shows a large public house with an entrance on the side. By 1933 Charles Webster had enlarged the beerhouse as the adjoining road, Raleigh Drive, was widened.

THE RISING SUN public house was built on the adjoining empty land and named by 1937. Interestingly in this period it was one of three inns in this short stretch of road. The full shape of the public house had appeared by 1933, but the name came later. The building is now the Tesco Express. Tesco stores now occupy many such sites in shopping areas. There are about six shops at this crossroads, so a convenience store at this point will be considered a useful addition and good investment for Tesco.

GAUMONT CINEMA, NORTH FINCHLEY

THE CINEMA, BUILT in the Art Deco style, opened in July 1937, showing Humphrey Bogart (then at the beginning of his career) in *The Black Legion*. It was designed by W.E. and W.S. Trent and officially opened by the mayor of Finchley, Alderman S. Pulham.

Its front curve was decorated with a magnificent frieze of Portland stone by Newbury Trent depicting the shooting of a film. The seating held 1,500 patrons in the stalls alone. Cinema in North Finchley was an exciting addition, bringing this area into the modern age. An Art Deco swimming pool was built nearby. Some large shops were also added to create a new shopping experience. The cinema held a prominent place on a centre island called 'the Tally Ho'. This site took its name from the coaching transport of an earlier period: one of the operating companies of the time was called the Tally Ho Coach Co.

THE GAUMONT CLOSED on 25 October 1980, the final film shown being the aptly named *The Last Picture Show*. The building was demolished in 1987. In the lengthy interim period, the space became a street market, creating a different type of retail outlet. The Arts Depot has successfully built its centre on the same lines as the former Gaumont, maintaining the curved frontage, but the current site is larger in volume – incorporating a covered bus depot, various theatre spaces, galleries, café, residential flats and rooms to hire.

FALLOW LODGE, No. 45 GRANVILLE ROAD, FINCHLEY

FREDERICK GOODYEAR WAS the first chairman of the newly formed Finchley Urban District Council in 1895. Before then, he was on the Finchley Local Board of 1882. He came to Finchley in 1849 and died at No. 45 Granville Road in 1937. He was a

straw-hat manufacturer and very active in local politics, coming into conflict with H.S. Stephens, also a very active local politician from East Finchley. The two men fell out over the question of sewerage (the infrastructure for removing waste). H.C. Stephen's father had manufactured the blue black Stephens' Ink. Sold in a glass bottle, the ink became a household commodity. The Stephens' Ink museum is nearby in Avenue House, East End Road.

THE LODGE WAS situated at Fallow Corner near the Wright-Kingsford homes for children, run by two charitable ladies of the same name. Blanche Wright and Ellen Kingsford were both trained nurses. The home was innovative in that it accepted children of unmarried mothers and was run entirely on voluntary support (the Shaftesbury Society being its sponsor). The house and Fallow Lodge were both demolished after the Second World War and replaced with much-needed housing.

PRIOR'S,
Nos 27 & 29
HIGH STREET,
NORTH FINCHLEY

THE OWNERS OF this large department store, opened in around 1880, appear in the 1881 census at No. 14 High Street, Finchley. Benjamin Prior, draper, employed five people (two draper's assistants were living in-house). The house was re-numbered in 1905 as Nos 27 and 29 High Street. The attractive Art Deco style was a later improvement: the building was splendidly decorated and added to the importance of North Finchley as a rising modern shopping centre. The store, and the Gaumont Cinema, marked the beginning of change in Finchley, one that residents were proud of.

THE SHOP WAS bombed in November 1940, and sadly the devastation was too great to attempt repair. It was decided to take another site nearby, on the corner of the High Street and Castle Road, the former site of Stephen's Memorial Hall at Nos 704-708 (re-numbered) High Road. Old Prior's was subsequently rebuilt and replaced by two retail shops. Tally Ho Discount and WHSmith's stationers are the current occupiers. North Finchley today remains a thriving shopping centre, probably the busiest in the borough.

THE GREEN MAN,
HIGH ROAD,
EAST FINCHLEY

THIS OLD INN was rebuilt several times, the last model being in 1935. It stood on Finchley Common, an area notorious for highwayman in an isolated spot on the road to Barnet and St Albans. Legendary highwaymen including Dick Turpin have been associated with the common, but there is little evidence to support these claims beyond a romantic notion. There were, however, high levels of thievery in the eighteenth

century, many such crimes being reported in the newspapers, and the area was avoided by travellers at night. The enclosure of the common in 1814 brought this problem to an end. The Inclosure of Commons, a national movement, was favourable for many areas, making undeveloped land available for occupation. However, people who relied on access to this common land to gather wood or fuel, or to graze their livestock, often suffered.

THE AREA BEHIND the inn was bought by the Regent's Canal Co. in 1811. They were intent on making a reservoir here, as this was a very 'watery' place, with Strawberry Brook running beside the inn and flowing into Brownswell on the opposite side of the road. In 1756 the War Office billeting returns show The Green Man as having room for three soldiers and their horses. Billeting was compulsory and often disliked by publicans – non-payment of keep for the soldiers was common. The building was finally demolished in 1993 when the North Circular Road was widened, with only a large open space now indicating where it had once stood, and little recognition of its contribution to East Finchley's history.

WHITE LION, HIGH STREET, EAST FINCHLEY

A PUBLIC HOUSE has stood at this strategic site for many centuries. This main thoroughfare from London was later known as the Great North Road. In the early 1800s coaches vied with each other for trade, racing the highways and shortening the distance between changes. The milestones were a measure of distance, each marking a mile, and were used for timing and for accuracy of pricing. A railway station, whose line terminated at Edgware, was built next to the White Lion in 1867, carrying the rail lines overhead by bridge. The route had already become a main stagecoach thoroughfare to London, and the area was an important part of the commuter belt. Anthony Salvin, the architect of Holy Trinity Church on East End Road in around 1849, and his family resided at Elmhurst House for

several years. A notebook kept by his daughter records their life there. It describes the transport to London provided by the coachmen, and the family's use of it before the building of the railway. It's a lovely revelation of domestic and professional life in the suburb. The public house was rebuilt at least three times, and a coloured engraving, after James Pollard, was engraved by G. Reeves in 1825. It depicts all the finery and pomp of wealthy travellers in this early period. The emblem of King George IV sits on the carriage door, a sign of the service's status.

TODAY AN ENLARGED pub continues to serve thirsty travellers. The building is overseen by the iconic Art Deco design of an archer by Eric Aumonier. Made in 1940, this figure stands over the station pointing in the direction of Central London. Just a few yards south of the station stands the now famous Bishop's Avenue, on land owned by the Bishop of London, with large houses once occupied by celebrities such as Gracie Fields, the Sultan of Brunei, Lakshmi Mittal and other well-known individuals.

GROVE HOUSE, No. 287 REGENTS PARK ROAD

THIS PHOTOGRAPH SHOWS a detached house at Finchley, on the main road near
St Mary's parish church, which is now called Grove Lodge. The Barrington-Baker family
lived here from 1877 to 1945, and papers and photographs dating from 1895 to 1925
were found in the house. They belonged to Dr James Barrington-Baker (*c.* 1895-1909),
and included a postcard sent to his wife. His son, James Barrington-Baker junior,

architect, enlarged and repaired a number of churches in north London, along with drafting plans for St Michael's church, Golders Green, and St Michael's, East Barnet. These plans, with others, are archived at Lambeth Palace Library. There is also a lovely photograph in the archive of the road widening undertaken here in the 1920s, and many professional photographs of the family too.

THE BUILDING APPEARED sometime after 1841 and was there on the first Ordnance Survey map of 1864. When the house was built there were no intrusions around it, and it had a spectacular view of the hill gently sloping down in the direction of Golders Green. Finchley Road leads out of John Nash's beautifully designed housing around Regents Park, first proposed for the Prince Regent in London and entering the borough at Childs Hill. From Golders Green the same road continued as Regents Park Road, a main thoroughfare out of London heading north. It has recently had considerable refurbishment, bringing this attractive house the attention it deserves on a prime site on the main road, in a central position to the station, parish church and shopping area.

FINCHLEY
MEMORIAL HOSPITAL,
FALLOW CORNER

A CHARMING STORY goes with the building in 1908 of this quaint hospital, then called
Finchley Cottage Hospital. At the turn of the twentieth century, Finchley, already
considerably populous, did not have many facilities for its population. The main facility
it lacked was a hospital: the nearest hospitals were in the north in Barnet Town, or
south at The Whittington in Islington. This situation was considered unacceptable for
a growing area. A group of concerned citizens engaged the community, and began to

raise the money to build such a useful amenity. Ebenezer Holman of Finchley donated the land on which it was to be built, and other contributors added financial support. The Finchley Carnival, still running today, was instigated in 1904 to raise money for the building. Through the years, it has provided the support to purchase extra beds and equipment.

AFTER THE FIRST World War, the population of the area grew rapidly and the local council decided to build an extension to the hospital as a memorial to those local men who had died in the war. An appeal was launched for funds, and by the beginning of the 1920s some £22,000 had been raised. It was re-named Finchley Memorial Hospital in commemoration. Due to the increasing number of road-traffic accidents (the hospital was located by two main roads), a casualty department was built in 1926. Extensions were added over the years. The original hospital building was demolished in 2012 and a large replacement took its place. The grounds fronting the former hospital will hopefully, if the plans come to fruition, soon be landscaped.

FINCHLEY
GARDEN VILLAGE,
VILLAGE ROAD

THE GARDEN-CITY movement brought an intriguing collection of concepts to urban planning, bringing together town and country in a carefully planned arrangement of housing and green spaces. One of the biggest in the borough was Hampstead Garden, but Finchley Garden in 1909 was certainly a unique arrangement in its own setting. Its location was on a gentle hill tapering down to Dollis brook and in its time it had a huge expanse of land beyond it (later called Windsor Open Space). The designer of this garden village was

Frank E. Stratton from the local firm of Bennett and Stratton, whose offices were at Finchley Central; they designed some cottage-style houses in pairs, each pair individually incorporating traditional rural architectural features. The houses were laid out around an informal green. Some of the houses were bought by family and friends, including Frank Stratton and his sister. Many communal celebrations took place on the green, and some lovely photographs, a legacy of these times, are now in the Local Studies' collection. Peggy Wells was the main instigator of these celebrations.

FINCHLEY CO-PARTNERSHIP SOCIETY built the houses for the 'less wealthy middle classes'. Stratton died in June 1922 and is commemorated by a memorial lamp, which also acts as a war memorial. Discovery of this well-hidden development comes as a delightful surprise; the houses are self contained within their own dedicated space, and are not on an access road. The story of this development is a very interesting one, and it is well worth investigating in more detail.

RITZ CINEMA, EDGWARE, STATION ROAD

THE RITZ WAS built on site of the rectory for St Margaret's, which was sold in 1919. Architect William James King originally named this cinema The Citadel in his design. He built it in Romanesque style, with simple bold stone courses designed to make it look like the citadel of its name. However, it was finally called The Ritz and had, as many cinemas did in the 1930s, an accompanying doorman. An impressive Compton organ and internal décor suggesting distant hills, valleys and wooded country (with nude

figures lost in the silvery mist) were to be found indoors, though they had gone by 1968. It opened on the May 1932 and had a seating capacity of 2,120. In the year of its opening, *Letty Lynton* was showing, with Joan Crawford and Robert Montgomery, a tale of love and blackmail. It was withdrawn in 1936 due to copyright arguments over the script used by MGM, which had clearly been plagiarised from a stage play of the time. *The Silent Voice* with George Arliss and Bette Davis was the B movie. Pathé News reels show well-dressed crowds queuing at the entrance in a film entitled *The Ritz – Edgware's wonderful new cinema – opens*. A fanfare played by smiling white-jacketed trumpeters welcomed visitors at the front doors. The Citadel Regency sign is displayed on one of the shops standing adjacent to the excited queues.

BY 1944 IT had become the ABC, and between 1993 and 1997 it was the Belle Vue, hosting Indian films for the Bollywood market. Ragu Patel and his cousin C.J. Patel bought the cinema in around 1995 and ran the first Indian cinema in England. The previous complex contained ten shops, each leased by Raymond's estate agents for £145 a year. The block was finally demolished in 2001, and a massive block of commercial buildings replaced it. The site is now occupied by Centurion House, a large building of mixed residency and commercial use.

THE FORUM,
HIGH STREET, EDGWARE

CHARLES WRIGHT ENGINEERS Ltd moved to Thornbank, Edgware, from Clerkenwell, London, in 1900 due to environmental and building changes in the city. Edgware was a quiet backwater, and was described as very rural – more so than usual for an area so close to London. The only modern amenity was a railway, built in 1864. The village's main

street was called Church Road until the coming of the tube in 1924, when the name was changed to Station Road. By 1910 the stretch all along the Edgware Road had sprouted with buildings of a semi-industrial nature. Charles Wright's were dye manufacturers who also produced medals, signs and other public insignia. The company had government contracts in the First World War, and produced a large number of war medals after it. (By 1960, the firm were engaged in providing car number plates.) The Forum was built in the 1930s, in a corner space a short distance from Thornbank backing on to the Edgware Station. Charles Wright, as a trustee, helped improve the fabric and added sculleries to the seventeenth-century almshouses in Mill Hill fronting the Angel Pond. Wright lived in Mill Hill and Totteridge till his death in 1938.

TODAY THE EDGWARE Road remains a wide expanse, clustered with remnants of these industrial buildings turned to other commercial uses – selling new cars, kitchen design and carpets. There is a lot of potential for development when finance becomes available; in addition, what needs further consideration is that the road is divided between two boroughs, with Edgware Road being the boundary marker between Brent and Barnet.

ST JAMES' SCHOOL, BURNT OAK

IT IS RARE for a house of this age (it was built in 1882) and type to have survived in Burnt Oak. The mock Gothic style, with its heavy decorative finish, flatters its overall design. The building is seen here in around 1927. Just a few years before, in 1924, the area saw huge developments due to the coming of the tube line. This changed what was an entirely agricultural landscape into a new suburb overnight. The house has been home to the rich and the celebrated: Claude Grahame-White, an aviation pioneer *extraordinaire* from 1912 to 1915, once lived here. He established one of the four premier aerodromes around London when he set up the Hendon Aerodrome. Attendance was phenomenal, including heads of state, industry and politics; the programmes invariably included some awe-inspiring aeronautic displays. The Royal Air Force was given his factory for the war effort in 1914. Today the RAF museum stands on the aerodrome site just to the south-east of the house.

THE HOUSE WAS next occupied by St Rose's Roman Catholic Convent from 1920 onwards. They built a large boys' school in its grounds, which covered 3 acres. The school ran from 1934 until 1980, when it moved to a new site opposite the RAF Museum. The provision of a school was vital to the expanding area: the local authority had underestimated the immediate need for school places. The house was re-named No. 1 Buckle Court, and its grounds dotted with several houses – the original building makes for an astonishing discovery, the house successfully hidden by high walls and a concealed front entrance. There have been some subtle changes to the exterior of the house, which has undergone some building expansion. This substantial building has today lost a little of its opulence, but it is still a proud remnant of its era.

WALFIELD, No. 1502 HIGH ROAD, WHETSTONE

WALFIELD WAS ACQUIRED by Henry W. Lazuan in 1796. It stood near the county boundary between Middlesex and Hertfordshire, north of Whetstone. Lazuan was a man of commercial importance who purchased, with Francois Charles Lauzan and Robert Charles Brohier, shares of the Schweppes Mineral Water Company (formed in 1783 by Jean Jacob Schweppe) for making and composing artificial mineral waters, a subject that had appealed to Bermudian 'mindral' drinkers. The Lauzans had lived in Jamaica, Guernsey, France and London, with commercial enterprises in each country. He appreciated the value of the mineral waters to the company's interests. He sold his house to raise money for purchasing the shares in around 1815, and retained the name Schweppes.

SCHWEPPES LTD MOVED into the borough of Barnet a century later due to space and environmental restrictions in London, where its main factory stood. The design of the house was most unusual, retaining a Continental style, and is remembered in this area as a symbol of industrial importance. The house was demolished in 1964 but the name survives as Walfield House and, on the opposite side, Walfield Avenue. Today this stretch of the High Road is dotted with many flats for the increasing borough's population.

THE CHAPEL, TOTTERIDGE LANE, WHETSTONE

THE CONGREGATIONAL CHAPEL, also known as Dissenters' Chapel, was built in 1827 as a mission for the poor by Catherine Puget of Totteridge, a Huguenot family who were munificent in supporting the local community. The building was set back from the road and included a burial ground. In 1810 Mrs Catherine Puget had also paid for a brick-built chapel in Totteridge Village intended for the use of the labourers on her estate; it is still here, though today it is known as Chapel Cottage and is a private dwelling. By 1828, a school had been added. William Golding was its first minister, but by 1897 it was registered as disused. A new church was opened in 1888

at the junction of Oakleigh Road North, Whetstone, called Christ Church, where services continued. Sitting in the dip of Totteridge Lane, half a penny was charged by a carrier to cross the Dollis Brook to the chapel.

IN 1919, AND leading up to the Second World War, the building was used as an automobile repair garage. In 1939 it was acquired by Borough of Barnet and became an Air Raid Precaution (ARP) centre. These centres were there to co-ordinate Civil Defence activities such as distribution of gas masks, responding to bomb incidents, providing transport to hospitals and the cutting off – if need be – or restoration of water, gas and electricity supplies. The deceased were exhumed and removed for re-burial at The Hendon Cemetery and Crematorium in 1991. The burial ground is a protected area and was therefore preserved, but the chapel was demolished and redeveloped in around 2000.

FENELLA HOUSE, THE BURROUGHS, HENDON

THIS HOUSE WAS built in 1887 by Hendon's GP James Cameron, who sadly died in a road accident in 1891. The name Fenella had associations with his home in Scotland. He served as an all-round medical practitioner for all of Hendon's population,

including the inmates of the local union workhouse at Burnt
Oak. The house was sold to Hendon Borough Council in
1934 for £4,250 by Dr Francis W. Andrews, who succeeded
Dr Cameron. It was later used by Hendon Council's Citizens
Advice Bureau from the 1950s until 1974. The Barnet Housing
Benefits' department moved in 1988 and vacated it in July 2008.
It appears this building was always in institutional occupation:
being almost opposite the Town Hall, it had a supportive function
to essential corporate services. Nearly all the buildings along The
Burroughs served some type of formal establishment: on one side
were Middlesex University, fire station, library and Town Hall;
and on the other, the White Bear Inn, methodist church, council
buildings and a large bus depot parallel with Fenella House.

FENELLA HOUSE WAS demolished and replaced by a functional
block of three-storey red brick, fit for purpose as Barnet's education
enquiries office. It stands opposite the magnificent new Middlesex
University extension: the university now owns the building.

PDSA,
No. 2 CHURCH ROAD, HENDON

THIS ATTRACTIVE BUILDING was built after the First World War and occupied in 1926 by J. Richards Ltd, dairy farmers, and by 1928 United Dairies, reflecting the semi-rural tradition of delivering milk to houses. In around 1970 the building was the People's Dispensary for Sick Animals (PDSA), an innovative free service that had started in 1917 in

Whitechapel. It provided care for the pets of people in economic need. The building was later occupied as a shop. It was demolished in 1976, and the building was replaced by social housing. It stands at the centre of the parish of Hendon, strategically built on the corner and with a thirteenth-century church within a few hundred yards, several almshouses and a school with much to offer in terms of architectural history.

IT HAS SEEN much change, as many of the older properties were replaced to accommodate a growing population. However, the change is not unsympathetic and has blended in well within a designated Conservation Area. A new PDSA premises was built behind it on a parallel road. The Claddagh Ring public house, formerly the Middlesex Hotel, sits next to it on Church Road with live bands, late-night openings and pavement seating. It is very popular, and also attracts neighbouring Middlesex University students. The Cricklewood district just south of the public house was a strong Irish community and still has many connections to the Barnet area.

ST SAVIOUR'S HOME, No. 19 BRENT STREET

IN AUGUST 1893 Reverend Seddon, secretary
of the evangelical group the Church Army,
bought Fosters, a large house on Brent Street.
He later built an adjacent building as St Saviour's
Homes for so-called 'feeble-minded' women
in 1897, with a chapel attached. The architects
were H.A. Prothero and G.H. Phillpot.
The Building News of June 1897 described this
new building. In 1926 it was taken over by the
Pillar of Fire Society as a bible college, school and
chapel. The new building was named after the
society's American founder, Alma White, as part
of a complex of buildings.

SERVICES WERE STILL being held here in 1994. Their own church doctrines would be more of a Methodist heritage. This Grade II building, encircling a secluded square, was redeveloped in 2009, by someone who appreciated the use and design of the building, as the Pillar Hotel and has function rooms for Jewish clients. The Jewish community are well represented in Hendon, Golders Green and Edgware. When Golders Green was created as a new suburb – literally on undeveloped open fields, with the building of an underground of the same name in 1907 – it attracted many families, and today remains the most populated Jewish area in London. (It also provides some excellent restaurants and bakeries.) The Jewish population has spread north to Hendon and Edgware. The building is still beautifully conserved, though hidden behind its main entrance, and is still arranged around a courtyard with an inner sanctum.

MIDDLESEX UNIVERSITY, THE BURROUGHS, HENDON

THE UNIVERSITY HAS undergone many curricular changes and institution names. It was built by the Middlesex County Council in 1937-39 as Hendon Technical Institute, renamed Hendon Technical College in 1945, and Hendon Institute of Technology in 1962. In 1973 it became part of Middlesex Polytechnic, which in 1992 became Middlesex University. This photograph was taken at its opening in September 1939 – though the official ceremony was cancelled due to the outbreak of war. It was prestigious that Hendon, created a borough in 1932, was providing higher education opportunities. Somewhat austere in design, with touches of Art-Deco style, it was one of the architectural decorations of The Burroughs.

IN 2005 THE inner entrance to the magnificent glazed Sir Raymond Rickett Quadrangle
was covered by remodelling the existing 1930s building by BPR Architects. It has
heightened the Art Deco style further, with a comparable artistic design covering
the inner forecourt. Several new buildings were added in the grounds. These have
consolidated many school buildings into the one complex, surrounded by fine
supporting buildings.

HATCHCROFT,
THE BURROUGHS,
HENDON

ON A 1754 map surveyed by Isaac Messeder and James Crow, 'Hatch Croft' is a piece
of land over 6 acres fronting a large house called Grove House, which faces The
Burroughs. It is mentioned in a conveyance in 1757 and in another in 1814, with an

accompanying map that shows the plot (with limited building area within it). In 1898 Doctor William Eldridge-Green conveyed Hatch Croft meadow to Doctor Henry Hicks of Grove House. Hatchcroft was built in 1900 by George Hornblower FRIBA. The design was exhibited at the Royal Academy the same year. Over the years this building has been engaged in council services of different kinds: its proximity to the Town Hall was beneficial to its use.

IN 2008 AN ambitious semi-glass design of outstanding quality and imagination replaced an equally attractive older building, demolished in 2007. The building neatly fits within the conservation limits and complements the older structure of Middlesex University next door. The Hatchcroft Building houses the majority of the university's science and social science programmes. It is designed by BPR Architects who had also worked on the modernised main building and was awarded 'excellent' BREEAM status by the Building Research Establishment, significantly exceeding current building regulations for achieving environmental sustainability.

WHITE BEAR,
THE BURROUGHS,
HENDON

THIS WAS A very old and attractive public house where manorial courts were frequently held for many centuries under the jurisdiction of the lord of the manor. It is here that courts were held until at least 1916. A blue plaque recognising its former

function as Court Leet and Court Baron is affixed at the front. The distinction between the two courts was that the former dealt with criminal matters, and the latter with domestic issues such as land and boundaries. Interestingly enough, the Bear Field lies behind this plot on the 1754 map by Isaac Messeder and James Crow, where both building and field are shown.

ITS STRATEGIC POSITION at the centre of the parish, and its legal functions, made this inn an important place for local activities and may have influenced the siting of the now prestigious Hendon Town Hall a few hundred yards away. It was rebuilt in 1932, with the front being set back from the road where previously the front line was in keeping with the rest of the buildings. It closed as a public house in 2007 and has had only temporary use since.

ODEON CINEMA, CHURCH ROAD/PARSON STREET JUNCTION, HENDON

THE ODEON, WITH its Art Deco design, had served Hendon since August 1939. The architect was H.W. Weedon FRIBA, and the building replaced cottages at Cook's Corner. Cook's were a building company, but perhaps the changing times precipitated the cinema's demise. This modern design replaced a popular cinema at the crossroads of the centre of Hendon's old village. As the village grew, so did custom go further afield: it was hoped the cinema would attract more people back to this area.

THE CINEMA WAS demolished and residential flats took its place, commanding an important position in the village. The crossroad here led to the important districts of Mill Hill to the north, Golders Green to the south and Finchley to the east. Its position was quite distinct, although other social factors may well have influenced its loss of use.

SACRED HEART CHURCH, THE BROADWAY, MILL HILL

THE CHURCH WAS built in 1923 and opened by Cardinal Bonno. The style was influenced by Byzantine, Egyptian and Roman influences, and particularly by the recent discovery of Tutankhamen's tomb in 1922. The architects were Father Benedict Williamson and J.H. Beart Foss, and the church had seating for 350 people.

IT WAS REBUILT in December 1994 and the modern design was quite a contrast. Mill Hill was considerably influenced by Roman Catholicism, as several institutions were to be found in The Ridgeway for more than a century when the town was still on the hill. New Mill Hill had migrated down to the flat plains, where two railway lines were built, in the late 1860s, and these plains provided better layout for shops, cinemas and other community activities. The position of Mill Hill did give it a sense of exclusivity and many of the residents here resorted to the use of carriages for transport in earlier times. Mill Hill is at the highest point in the Middlesex range, and during the Second World War a cricket ground here was taken over by the army for use as a gun emplacement.

DOWNHURST SCHOOL, PARSON STREET, HENDON

THIS EXTRAORDINARY BUILDING was used by The Hasmonean Grammar School which was founded in 1944 as a co-educational school in The Drive, Golders Green, by Rabbi S. Schonfeld, principal of the Jewish Secondary Schools' Movement. In 1947

the boys moved to Ravensfield, The Burroughs, which was later extended and had 465 pupils in 1969, when the school was voluntary aided. In 1952 the girls, all from Orthodox Jewish families, left Golders Green for Downhurst, a former private school called Downhurst School for Girls. The school had been there since 1926, and was formerly, before 1911, a private residence. The school was later extended and had 289 pupils by 1974. They moved again to a purpose-built school in Page Street, Mill Hill, in 1975, where they remain today.

THE JEWISH POPULATION had increased tremendously, forming part of a new suburb in Golders Green with the coming of the tube line in 1907, building synagogues, social institutions and a network of supporting structures in the surrounding area. Today, No. 49 Downhurst Court is a block of residential flats standing on the former site of the school.

MIDLAND HOTEL, STATION ROAD, HENDON

THE HOTEL CERTAINLY entertained a range of guests alighting from the railway station next door. The station was built in 1867. The design has seen very little change, and that mostly cosmetic. Here it was that pedestrian visitors would have alighted for the Grahame White Aerodrome, there being no other station nearby.

THE STATION'S POSITION on the slope of the hill gave it a spectacular view of the aerodrome in the early twentieth century. In order to view aerodrome activities, many locals would sit on top of Hendon Hill, where the parish church stands, to get a good view free of charge. Certainly the aerodrome was the most exciting institution of its time and huge numbers of people – royalty, heads of the Armed Forces, personalities of stage and politics – would visit. Flying was truly one of the wonders of the age.

THE IONIC, FINCHLEY ROAD, GOLDERS GREEN

THE AREA GREW suddenly with the building of the new tube line from Hampstead to Golders Green over the near-impossible range of Northern Heights' hills, a build enabled by a new type of underground tunnelling introduced by Charles Tyson Yerkes, an American. Designed by William James King, a Hendon builder and councillor, it was executed in Monks Park stone from Bath, Wiltshire, with seating for 700 visitors. The area benefited from many new amenities. The Ionic, just one of these, was of Grecian style with four columns above fronting a standard square building. The Golders Green Hippodrome nearby was an impressive theatre and together they provided excellent recreational choice.

THE IONIC WAS opened in 1913 by the dancer Anna Pavlova, who lived nearby who lived nearby at Ivy House, North End Road, Golders Green (today the London Jewish Cultural Centre). It attracted a number of audiences, but was finally demolished in 1975. It was replaced with another theatre of the same name, albeit with a much more sober design. Again, this building was recently cleared as the adjacent Sainsbury's took over its premises as an extension.

POLICE STATION, TEMPLE FORTUNE, GOLDERS GREEN

THE STATION WAS built after the First World War and by 1926 was numbered 1069 Finchley Road. This road, which led from Marble Arch to Finchley, was built under an Act of 1826. The area then grew tremendously in 1907 with the coming of the tube line from Hampstead, a marvellous engineering feat brought about by an American entrepreneur called Charles Tyson Yerkes. Yerkes was involved with Chicago's public transportation system and similar projects before his involvement in London's underground. In 1900, on making observations from Hampstead Heath, he set up a tube line under the Underground Electric Railways Company, creating two lines from Charing Cross, which was later called the Northern Line. The tube line caused a tremendous growth in population, and houses rapidly sprung up where formerly only a few dwellings stood.

A GROWING COMMUNITY was in need of formal structural support such as a police station, and to this end one was built at Temple Fortune. It still functions as such, wedged between many shops in a busy shopping parade.

MIDLAND TERRACES, CRICKLEWOOD

MIDLAND, GRATTON, JOHNSTON, Needham, Campion. A charming group of terraces were built for railway workers of the Midland Railways in the 1860s. The station was originally known as 'Childs Hill and Cricklewood', and opened in 1867. The first set of cottages south of the station fronted the Edgware Road (whose names are taken

from members of the Midland's railway board). The company extended the line from Hampstead in 1864 to Cricklewood, at that time a rural area with only the Edgware Road or Watling Street running through from Marble Arch. The 4 mile stone marking the distance from London stood opposite Gratton Terrace, a reminder of a time when coaching was the dominant form of public transport. Watling Street, the long road from London which has now been mostly re-named, was a Roman road. Pottery kilns were excavated on the road north of this site, near Edgware, in the 1950s.

AWARE OF THE isolated nature of the area, the company provided open greens and individual gardens for their employee's enjoyment. The terraces have been maintained as they originally were, and protected and celebrated for retaining their industrial history. Until 1952 all the roads to these terraces were private: a gate was closed one day in the year to ensure this, but now the roads have been adopted by Barnet Council and are no longer private.

CRICKLEWOOD
AERODROME

AERIAL POWER BEGAN in Hendon in 1910. Frederick Handley Page, aeronautic engineer at Cricklewood in 1912, moved to the area soon afterwards. His contribution to producing fighter planes was remarkable. Queen Alexandra, on a visit in March 1918, seemed surprised at the number of women employed in the production processes. During the First World War a large number of planes were manufactured here, and the number of people in the workforce was phenomenally high. However, numbers slumped immediately after the war, dropping from around 5,000 to 100 employees. Many aircraft companies were unable to change direction, having become reliant on government contracts,

and had folded. Handley Page developed a prototype bomber capable of overseas flight in 1915. One night, late in December 1915, the first prototype twin engine biplane with bomb carrier was assembled in Kingsbury and wheeled down Edgware Road along the tram lines, with folded wings, to Hendon Aerodrome. The overhead tram wires and gas lamps had been removed in advance under Admiralty orders and, to the annoyance of local residents, the tree branches that got in the way.

AFTER THE WAR – and a few financially unsuccessful starts – Page set up Imperial Airways in 1924 in Cricklewood. With government subsidies, it was one of the first public airlines and the direct predecessor to what became British Airways. An aerodrome behind the factory at Cricklewood was purchased by the Crown to aid the development of planes and closed in 1929 (though the factory manufacture continued). In the Second World War Handley Page made the now famous Halifax bombers. A housing scheme, seen here, was sympathetically designed to cover a very large area that was the aerodrome.

THE CROWN, BROADWAY

THIS INN STOOD on The Edgware Road near the southern corner of Cricklewood Lane. It further progressed as an inn with the building of the Childs Hill and Cricklewood railway in 1867. The road from London was formerly turnpiked in 1712 and saw a lot of traffic, being a straight Roman road from Marylebone to Edgware and beyond to St Albans, an old Roman town and a place of pilgrimage. The road's maintenance was paid for by turnpike payments, though complaints were often made regarding the ground, which was frequently near-impassable in the wet season. In 1736 the licensee was John Rush. He was entered in the Hendon Parish vestry minutes. The previous building dates back at least to the middle of the eighteenth century. One Mrs Harriott Mencelin was responsible for the rates of the Crown Ale House, with 23 perches of land, in the 1796 John Cooke map. An identical building may be seen on the 1754 Isaac Messeder map.